**Level 1** is ideal for children who have received some initial reading instruction. Stories are told, or subjects are presented very simply, using a small number of frequently repeated words.

## Special features:

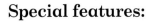

Amazing trains!

fast train

pass

train full of cars

new train    steam train

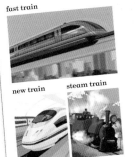

8

9

Large, clear labels and captions

**Trains full of goods**
Trains can take goods, like cars or coal, as well as passengers.

Careful match between text and pictures

cars

This goods train is full of cars.

goods train

coal

This goods train is full of coal.

14

15

Educational Consultant: Geraldine Taylor

Book Banding Consultant: Kate Ruttle

Subject Consultant: Ian Graham

LADYBIRD BOOKS

UK | USA | Canada | Ireland | Australia
India | New Zealand | South Africa

Ladybird Books is part of the Penguin Random House group of companies
whose addresses can be found at global.penguinrandomhouse.com.

www.penguin.co.uk  www.puffin.co.uk  www.ladybird.co.uk

First published 2017
001

Copyright © Ladybird Books Ltd, 2017

Printed in China

A CIP catalogue record for this book is available from the British Library

ISBN: 978-0-241-27548-1

All correspondence to
Ladybird Books
Penguin Random House Children's Books
80 Strand, London WC2R 0RL

# Amazing
# Trains

Written by Catherine Baker
Illustrated by Martin Sanders

# Contents

# Amazing trains!

## fast train

## new train

## steam train

## passenger train

## train full of cars

# A train trip

If you want to go on a trip, you can take a train.

This train is taking people on holiday.

**passengers**

11

# Trains at work

Look at all these trains!

The trains are taking people to work.

These trains are full of passengers.

# Trains full of goods

Trains can take goods,
like cars or coal, as well
as passengers.

goods train

**cars**

This goods train is full of cars.

**coal**

This goods train is full of coal. 15

# Steam trains

Look at this old train.

People go on a trip on this train.

**steam**

This old train is a steam train.

17

# New trains

## These new trains look amazing!

These people are going on holiday.

19

These people are going to work.

# Fast trains

If you want a fast trip, take a train like this!

Can you see all the people going on the fast passenger train?

fast train

# Underground trains

These trains are taking people on a trip underground!

Many people go to work on underground trains as well.

underground
train

23

# Up and down on the train

Old trains can take you up hills and down hills.

You can have an amazing trip going up and down hills

# Amazing train trips

You can go on amazing trips on . . .

. . . a steam train.

. . . an underground train.

. . . a fast train.

. . . a new train.

# Picture glossary

 fast train

 goods train

 new train

 old train

 passengers

 passenger train

 steam train

 underground train

# Index